Last Nerve

℘

What's Driving Your Office Crazy and What to Do About It

by
Dale Collie

TRUE NORTH PUBLISHING
CHARLOTTE BEIJING KIEV VANCOUVER

Last Nerve

ॐ

What's Driving Your Office Crazy and What to Do About It

by
Dale Collie

Published by True North Publishing
EAN 9781449918347
ISBN 1449918344

Published by True North Publishing
Charlotte   Beijing   Kiev   Vancouver

Printed in the United States of America

Dedication and Acknowledgments

Dedication

Last Nerve is dedicated to all of the hard working, often unrecognized office workers who make our businesses succeed.

Acknowledgments

Recognition is given to the many people who called and emailed these questions as a result of weekly interviews on Bridgeport, CT radio station WICC.

A special thanks also goes to Karen Ginn for editing and proofreading, to Steve Collie for cover design and graphics, and to Asher Telleen Collie (Eden Photography) for author's photo.

About the Author

Dale Collie is a full-time author and professional speaker, using the leadership skills of US Army Rangers to help key people succeed in tough times.

Dale was the first university graduate in his family, the first to break from his agrarian heritage, and the first to choose a military career as a US Army Ranger. He is also the first Vietnam Era infantry officer permitted to continue on active duty as an amputee.

Subsequent employment found him at the executive level in Fortune 500 companies. *Fast Company* business magazine recognizes Dale as one of America's Top 50 innovative leaders for his turn-around leadership of a bankrupt charity which re-stabilized financially and with Dale's leadership expanded nation-wide as a hunger relief organization and internationally as Dale started businesses in Eastern Europe to employ the impoverished and support orphanages.

Because of his experience in leadership control of workplace stress, McGraw-Hill contracted with him to write and publish *Winning under Fire: Turn Stress into Success the US Army Way,* now available in English, Russian, Chinese. The book *Last Nerve* developed from weekly radio interviews with one of the Northeast's major radio stations.

Contact Dale Collie for programs using the leadership skills of US Army Rangers to help key people succeed in tough times.

www.sn.im/contact-dale
www.CourageBuilders.com

Contents

Notes

Introduction

A United Nations' study tells us that workplace stress is an epidemic worldwide. The stress that is often the source of headaches and backaches can lead to much worse health conditions and cost our companies a lot of money.

Some reports advise that stress is the root cause of 60 to 90% of all doctor visits[1]. Another report explains that all of this health care and stress cost companies as much as 45% of bottom line profits when everything is considered—health care costs, personnel turnover, complaints, accidents, worker's comp, lowered productivity, and so on[2].

High stress levels affect both individuals the organization itself.

Corporate leadership can do a lot to control the stressors that lead to these big expenses. Management can make sure that workloads are balanced and that individual recognition is a high priority. Open communications can help reduce some of the stress. And confidence levels can be improved through proper training and work assignments.

In addition to the traditionally recognized causes of workplace stress, individuals often tell us that their main stressors are pet peeves that truly affect their

---

[1] *Perkins, A. (1994). Saving money by reducing stress. Harvard Business Review. 72(6):12.*
[2] 1990 study by the Princeton, NJ, benefits consulting firm of Foster Higgins & Co.

productivity—the clicking of a ball point pen, constant interruptions, lack of organization, to name a few.

These day-to-day irritants can cost your company a lot of money and add to the overall stress load that is affecting productivity.

Management is just as responsible for controlling these "pet peeves" as it is for developing a newsletter to communicate with employees. Leaders are just as responsible for controlling these daily irritants as they are for managing pay levels.

Each of the situations noted in *Last Nerve* comes from real life examples, either observed in my own forty years of leadership experience or from a popular radio program where I answered listener questions about workplace pet peeves.

Human Resources experts can guide you on whether the solutions offered are "legal" and whether they fit the policies of your company. As usual, don't do anything without consulting with your in-house experts.

You'll find advice on what employees should do if someone's constant pen clicking bothers them. There's advice for the employee who thinks there's too much work to do and for those who don't have enough work.

Individuals can read this book straight through or scan the table of contents to find specific problems they want to resolve.

Managers can draw from this book as they coach individuals, or they can select specific areas of advice to communicate with all employees by newsletter, email, memos, or whatever the chosen method of communication.

Management should keep in mind that using multiple channels of communication is more effective than using a single communication process.

Experience shows that using three or four methods of communicating the idea is more effective than any one of the ideas used alone. It's important to appeal to each of the learning styles if we want to maximize the effect of our communication.

Team leaders who want to advise people on how to handle someone who is always argumentative would want to post the information on the bulletin board, send a memo to each person on the team, cover the subject in the newsletter, and discuss it in a group meeting. Alternatives are to include the same information in emails and audio and video recordings. Successful leaders often use three or more communication styles for each item they want everyone to learn.

Common sense is the key for many of the topics included here and for the advice given. However, situations vary so much from state to state and company to company, you'll be well served in consulting your legal experts and human resources team before taking action on any of these suggestions.

One machine can do the work of fifty ordinary people. No machine can do the work of one extraordinary person.
[Elbert Hubbard]

Not Enough Work

I just don't have enough to do when I'm at work. Business isn't slow, but my job doesn't even fill the day. I spend a lot of time playing solitaire on the computer just waiting for time to clock out. I told my boss that I'm capable of more, but so far, it's just more solitaire. What can I do about this?[1]

Many people claim they have too much work and never get caught up, but an interesting twist heard from a number of frustrated employees is that there isn't enough work to fill their workdays.

People are very stressed when they are capable of more than the responsibilities they are given. They feel unappreciated and undervalued, and there is a lot of job insecurity involved. Be sure to give everyone the amount of work they can handle, or they are vulnerable to job turnover just like the overworked employees.

If you are the one without enough work to do, let your boss know that you're interested in more responsibilities.

Volunteer for extra projects. Use your annual review as a time to discuss this matter. If things don't change, you'll be attracted to another job opportunity—good for you, but bad for your employer.

---

[1] Questions in italics at the beginning of each section reflect real-life questions asked by employees.

Don't agonize. Organize.
[Florynce Kennedy]

Organize Your Desk Top

My desk is buried under work. I know I can work better if things are cleaned up, but how can I ever get my desk cleared?

1. Go through your stuff and make 3 stacks

    a. Stuff that must be done - the boss is expecting it

    b. Stuff that would be nice to do - I'd like to do it

    c. Everything else - junk and important but will never get to it.

2. Take all the "nice to do stuff" and put it in a box under your desk or somewhere out of sight in your office. Put everything in here that you're expected to do but no one ever checks.

3. Work only on the stuff that must be done; stuff the boss is expecting. In thirty days, go back to that second box of stuff that qualifies for the "you'd like to do it," and you'll find that you can throw most of it away.

4. Take the third box, the stack of stuff that doesn't fit into the first two categories, and throw it away. If that makes you too nervous, tape the box and store it. Get it out of your office.

Good people are hard to find. If you have extraordinary employees, do all you can to keep them.
[Dale Collie]

Good People Are Leaving

We're seeing co-workers switch jobs for promotions or to make more money. What can companies like ours do to hold onto key people?

5 Essentials for Keeping Good People

1. Make sure employees know they are appreciated.

2. Analyze your training programs and make sure people have the equipment needed for the job.

3. Distribute the workload to make sure you don't have underworked or overworked employees.

4. Help people feel like they're in control of their job and their lives.

5. Make sure management has good leadership and interpersonal skills.

6. Acquire a survey of prevailing wages in your area and make sure your company is competitive with the pay in other companies.

7. Find out who is hiring your departing co-workers and determine what those companies are doing differently.

8. Conduct exit interviews and get an accurate explanation as to why each co-worker is leaving.

You must be proactive to get a promotion.
You can waste years hoping that others
recognize the good work you do.
[Dale Collie]

Stuck in my job

I feel like I'm stuck in my job. Promotions come and go, but I'm always left behind. How can I get out of this rut and climb the ladder of success?

Discuss this with your boss as soon as possible. Find out what's holding you back and what you can do to overcome it.

Listen to what the boss says. Don't be offended.

Make a plan to work through this problem at your current company, or make plans to change jobs.

Remember, though, if you change jobs, you'll probably have the same limitations. Consider the boss' critique in an objective way. Ask friends for advice on this information.

Instead of complaining about the "negative" things you hear from your boss, decide to make the changes necessary to get that promotion you want.

Even though the work stops, expenses run on.
[Cato the Elder, 234 BC—149 BC]

Low Tech Boss

My boss really isn't up to speed on computer capabilities. The right software would get our work done faster and with fewer errors, but all he sees is the price of the software. How do I convince him that this is an investment in the company and in productivity?

Your boss probably sees that work is currently being accomplished with things as they are and asks, "Why spend money on gimmicks?"

- First, document current problems and errors and the cost of these problems.

- Determine the savings available with the new program.

- Get testimonials from others who are using the newer program (real numbers, not just enthusiastic comments).

- Consider contacting the program's sales rep; they should have ROI (return on investment) information readily available. To avoid angering the boss or frustrating the rep, make sure they both know that you are only exploring the program without authority to purchase.

- And ... (this could be the most important thing to understand) ... the boss might see this purchase as an expense instead of an investment. The key thing here is for you to do the job you're hired for. You get paid the same amount per hour whether you're using 20th Century or 21st Century tools.

Since more people are afraid of public speaking than of death, you're probably better off in the casket at a funeral than giving the eulogy.
[Jerry Seinfeld—paraphrased]

Fear of Public Speaking

I'm scared to death of public speaking, but the boss says I have to give a presentation standing in front of my coworkers and others. It doesn't matter to the boss whether I get hives and upset stomach and almost faint. Any tips on how to survive this?

Yes, the bottom line here is for you to "Get over it." It isn't easy to get beyond these obstacles, but if you want to get ahead, you're going to have to find a way to do the job. Speaking in front of groups is a key communications tool used in all businesses.

Take action now to get beyond this problem because your fear of public speaking (or your overcoming this problem) will have a huge effect on your success in the business world.

The fear is real, but you can overcome it with appropriate professional help.

- Enroll in a public speaking class

- Get individual coaching

- Join Toast Masters or other groups

If your company won't pay for the public speaking training and education, pay for it yourself. This is an important and necessary skill for you in your current and future jobs.

The difference between an allergy and an itch is about one hundred bucks.
[Anonymous]

Perfume at Work

My company just issued a policy against perfume, cologne, and aftershave lotion at work because one person claims to be allergic to the aromas. I'm getting fed up with people telling me how to act, how to dress, and now, how to smell. What can we do about it?

If you don't like this policy, you'll want to dust off your resume. Some people are allergic to the ingredients of some perfumes, and the company must take action to give them a safe place to work.

There are three solutions to this problem. The first is to fire the person with the allergy. The second is to isolate them at work. And the third solution is to ask everyone to cooperate in not bringing the aromas into the workplace.

For sure, no one is going to get fired because they are allergic, so management must decide what works best for the individual as well as for the company.

Don't forget the potential liability a company incurs if they ignore this problem. And consider how you'd feel if you had a similar situation and no one in management gave you the attention you deserve.

You're just going to have to go along with the company's no perfume policy. Don't waste anymore time complaining or talking among your fellow employees; you're not going to change things on this topic.

Courage is fire, and bullying is smoke.
[Benjamin Disraeli]

Boss is a Bully

My boss is a bully. He yells at us for very minor things. He throws papers back at some people when he's irritated. He curses to no end. Something must be bothering him at home, but he takes it out on all of us here in the office. We're tired of it, but we don't know what to do about this jerk???

Your boss isn't going to change. People who exhibit these characteristics are usually very insecure, in spite of the gruff demeanor they display. Their focus is on control, ego, and self-absorption.

They feel good when others suffer. They enjoy being called mean. There is no guilt or embarrassment about their actions.

While many bullies have a warm side and a winning smile to smooth over the injuries they cause, even *that* is a way of manipulating others.

If you are getting what you want from the job, grin and bear it. If the boss' attitude really bothers you, find another job.

If everyone would quit working for these bullies at the same time, management would have to take action and get rid of them, but most employees lack the confidence to quit en masse, so these jerks continue through life abusing others.

You'll have to make this decision on your own. Trying to get others to go with you is usually a waste of time and might affect your job search.

Decide whether to stay or go and either accept the rude behavior or prepare your resume. (Make sure you have a job lined up before quitting the old one).

Do your own job!
[Dale Collie]

People Aren't Doing Their Jobs

Some people in my office just don't do their jobs the way they should be done. They are late with their projects. Some of the information is incorrect, and they have a bad attitude about the company. What should I do about this?

It's easy to see that you're concerned about their productivity and how some workers' lack of effort affects the company. You have a good work ethic and know that success requires the best from all team members.

If these slackers reported to you, you'd take action to correct their behavior, but you're not the boss.

The bottom line is that you were not hired to observe or comment on the work habits of others. You have a job to do, and the boss of the slackers might not like your interference. As a matter of fact, your negative remarks about the workers can also be seen as a critique of their boss' ability to lead.

Unless these projects directly affect your own work, you should stick to what you're hired for and let the boss manage these people. Stick to your own job.

A minute of organization is worth an hour of chaos.
[Anonymous]

Cube-Mate is a Slob

The guy who shares the office cubicle with me never puts anything away or cleans his desk. It's a wreck, with stuff piled more than two feet high—no exaggeration! I'm no neat freak, but his place is making me nervous. He refuses to clean it up no matter how many times I mention it to him. What should I do?

Pay attention to your own workspace and forget about trying to manage other people.

This arrangement probably does affect you mentally and physically. The disorganization probably adds to your workplace stress.

However, guiding your co-workers work habits isn't your concern. When you become manager, you can establish the standards for neatness.

Neat doesn't mean the same thing to everyone, and your compulsion for order and organization might be alarming to the other person. If the company wanted you to be the manager of neat, they would have put that in your job description.

You shouldn't waste any more energy or let this situation affect your own productivity. It isn't worth an ulcer.

Some companies need a direction finder more
than they need GPS device.
[Dale Collie]

Company Lacks Direction

It seems like our company doesn't know where it's going. We work hard every day, but we're spinning our wheels while the competition eats our lunch.

Experience shows that employees are much more productive if management keeps them informed about company goals, activities, and problems.

It's hard to get everyone to pull together if they don't even know which direction they are going. Company leadership should communicate regularly about products, customers, opportunities, and the competition.

Everyone should be candid about immediate problems and what forecasts show. There are times when information must be guarded, but employees should be told about everything that isn't "top secret."

Not all managers agree with this concept. Other than making available some articles to illustrate the importance of an "open management" style, there is little you can do to convince these managers.

Keep in mind that you are an employee and that you are not managing the company. Unless you are planning to change jobs, don't make an issue of this.

You've been hired to take care of specific responsibilities. Pay attention to your own work, and make sure you're doing the best job possible with what you have.

No one ever listened themselves out of a job.
[Calvin Coolidge]

Headsets and Ear Buds

Everyone in my office is wearing headsets or ear buds. I never know when they're listening to music or paying attention to what I'm saying—even my boss! They seem to be getting their work done, but this electronic craze is driving me crazy. Any ideas?

Have a conversation with those you interact with most often.

Discuss how the headsets make you feel and listen to their reasons for wearing these obstacles to communication

Be understanding of their wishes, just as you would like for them to understand you.

You might be surprised to learn that they wear the headsets to reduce the number of interruptions they encounter on a daily basis (and you might find out that you are one of those recurring interruptions)!

They're probably unaware that the headsets make them unapproachable, so work out some kind of agreement.

If they're available all the time, they won't mind your getting their attention while they're wearing the headsets.

If they prefer that you use some kind of appointment schedule, you can work out some specific times that you'll engage them in conversation about business matters. In this way, a compromise might be reached without sacrificing effective communications.

Positive thinking will let you do everything better than negative thinking.
[Zig Ziglar]

Negative During Interview

I just interviewed someone who seems to be well qualified. During the interview, the person said some very negative, unsolicited things about a previous boss. As a matter of fact, negative remarks were made about several earlier managers. Should this affect my decision about hiring this person?

Negativity seems to be a part of this person's character, and you'll find the same attribute in your office if you put someone like this on your payroll.

Here are some things you'll have to decide:

- How do your other employees get along with each other?

- Is there a lot of negativity among those who already work there?

- How do you rate teamwork among current employees?

- Did you feel like you would be comfortable working with the interviewee?

If you already work in a negative environment, you'll be adding another negative thinker to the group. If your team is cooperative and usually positive, you should think twice before poisoning the atmosphere with the person you describe.

The interviewee might be a superb employee in completing tasks, but their negativity will affect others in your office.

Don't hire people for their potential. Hire them
for their proven ability.
[Dale Collie]

Hiring Mistake

We hired a new manager a few weeks ago, and we're starting to have second thoughts about it. His harsh personality is nothing like what we saw during interviews. Should we try to straighten him out, or should he seek employment elsewhere?

The boss of this individual should have a conversation about the differences you're seeing and give him a chance to get in step.

You might find that others are to blame for this "character" change that concerns you. Perhaps other employees are making the new person feel unwelcome. Maybe there are situations at home that affect the behavior you've observed.

Discuss the situation with your HR professional, and take action. Either this person provides what he was hired for, or you get someone else. HR will probably advise you to keep written memorandums concerning each conversation on this topic.

Do not let the situation go unresolved or everyone will suffer, including the bottom line. This is one of those things that will not correct itself.

It is impossible to enjoy idling thoroughly unless
one has plenty of work to do.
[Jerome K. Jerome]

More Work Right at Quitting Time

My boss has a habit of bringing me new projects just before quitting time. Often, I have to get the work done before I go home, and she waves good bye as she heads out the door. How can I get her to bring me these jobs in the middle of the work day?

Approach your boss around 1:30 or 2:00 p.m. and explain that you have some commitments that require you to leave on time today.

Ask whether she has anything that needs your attention, and let her know you'll complete the work before you go or first thing in the morning.

Obviously, you don't object to an occasional last minute requirement because urgent things happen in business all the time.

If the boss comments on your effort to rearrange your schedule, make sure she knows that you're all for the company and that you'll go the extra mile when there is a true emergency, but you're trying to improve your own time management so you accomplish more.

However, if this is the boss' way of squeezing an extra few hours of work from you each week (with or without pay), you'll need to regain control of your schedule or open your eyes to opportunities elsewhere.

Hard work never killed anybody,
but why take a chance?
[Edgar Bergen aka *Charlie McCarthey*]

Everyone Else is Getting Ahead

Some of my coworkers get all the advantages, and I get left behind. It really gripes me to see them get the special trips and seminars while I stay here and do the grunt work.

Perhaps you're just not yet qualified for the perks, or perhaps your co-workers are more socially savvy than you are. It will be easy for your boss to explain all of this if being left out is because of qualifications. The discussion will be much more difficult if it has to do with your ability to fit in.

Watch how the others interact with the boss and other departments. Are they schmoozing while you're objecting to the way things are done? Are they enthusiastic and gregarious while you're reclusive?

Ask your boss what you'll need to change to get those opportunities and promotions. Maybe the annual evaluation would be a good time to ask this question. Here are some more ideas:

5 ways to jump start your status in the company

1. Take a public speaking course - join Toastmasters.

2. Get someone to evaluate your appearance. Find out how to dress for corporate success.

3. Enroll in some additional skill training or education.

4. Stay up-to-date on your company and industry—read the journals.

5. Volunteer for projects. Start with the low-end, nobody wants to do this stuff, and work your way up. Grab every chance to research and present reports to the higher ups.

No man needs a vacation so much as
the man who has just had one.
[Elbert Hubbard]

Vacation Stress

My employees are so stressed about getting ready for vacation they don't even enjoy being away...too much to get ready and too much travel hassle. Is there any way I can help them get past this stress and make the entire vacation an enjoyable experience?

Here are some ideas for the boss.

1. Meet with employees two weeks before vacation to talk about their plans and set some goals for what must be done before their departure.

2. Encourage vacation savings throughout the year.

3. Invite a travel agency to your company for a lunchtime session on what's hot and what it's going to cost...negotiate some discounts for your employees as well.

4. Have a class on managing email and voice mail while on vacation.

5. Share the workload so employees are not overwhelmed when they return.

6. Give ½ day off before vacation for employees who meet the goals you helped establish two weeks before vacation.

7. Give each vacationing employee a $50 gas card on the way out the door.

I like buying snacks from a vending machine because food is better when it falls. Sometimes at the grocery, I'll drop a candy bar so that it will achieve its maximum flavor potential.
[Anonymous]

Vending Machine Food

Our company just announced a change in our break room vending machines. They're taking out my favorite stuff and putting in some fresh fruit. What business is it of theirs if I want a honey bun?

Even if your snack of choice is a honey bun, there's good medical evidence telling us that there are better things for both improved energy and lower calories.

Here are some things to consider.

- Have you given fruit a chance to work for you as a snack?

- Have you tried staying away from the sweets for a week?

- Have you discussed your cholesterol and triglyceride levels with your doctor?

- How is your weight and physical condition?

Your decisions about snack foods might be influenced by your response to any one of the above.

Because medical costs are soaring, management has an obligation to be involved in decisions about snack machine food. While the company isn't responsible for your health, your health can have a major impact on medical claims, missed work, and productivity.

Proper nutrition can influence workplace stress, and stress accounts for 60-90% of all doctor's visits.

If a honey bun is important to you, bring it from home, but listen to the health and nutrition advice about eating properly. You might be surprised at how much better fresh fruit serves your needs.

Vacation is what you take when you can't take what
you've been taking any longer.
[Anonymous]

Boss Complains About People Taking Time Off

I'm in management, and I'm fed up with all the holidays, vacations, sick leaves, and maternity leaves that we have to put up with. Every time I turn around, my employees are either gone or they're planning on going. How are we supposed to get any work done around here?

There seems to be an attitude problem at your company. The holidays, vacations, and other planned absences are part of the compensation package and part of the company's plan to maintain productivity.

Without the time away, stress levels continue to climb and productivity goes down. Illness increases. Turnover becomes a problem. All of these problems can be reduced or eliminated by proper leadership.

Complaining about these planned absences is a reflection on your own ability to get the work done on a planned basis.

Take a look at the calendar and get a staff of sufficient size to handle the workload. Hire some temp staff to handle the load while people are gone or hire some full-time people to make sure the work gets done.

And please don't let the staff hear you complaining about your *giving* them benefits they have *earned*. You'll reduce productivity and kill morale. And if you are too brash about this topic, you might end up hiring an entirely new staff.

What is the shortest word in the English language that contains the letters: abcdef?

Feedback—Don't forget that feedback is one of the essential elements of good communication.

[Anonymous]

No Feedback—Ever

What should I do to get my boss' attention? He never gives me any feedback on how I'm doing. I don't know whether he's very happy with my work or whether I'll be fired tomorrow. This lack of communication makes me very uncomfortable.

Have a meeting with your boss to talk about this.

If a lunch meeting is possible, the informal setting will take the edge off of your remarks.

If a lunch meeting isn't feasible, try going to the boss' office, but make sure you have an appointment so you won't be interrupted by other walk-ins or the telephone.

Explain that you are uncertain about how your work matches company expectations. Find out whether you can get feedback on a regular basis—weekly or monthly.

Your situation is more common than you might think. Many managers and leaders just don't realize the importance of keeping their teams informed about how their work is perceived. Many bosses have insufficient time to lead or manage properly because the "flat management structure" has too many people reporting directly to them.

If the boss thinks your concerns are unfounded and is reluctant to schedule a time for feedback, ask whether it is ok for you to ask for feedback on specific items from time to time and pepper the boss with questions until you get the feedback you need.

You can tell a lot about a fellow's character
by his way of eating jellybeans.
[Ronald Reagan]

Slobs at the Lunch Table

Some of the people who work here are just slobs when they eat in the break room or the cafeteria: forks used as scoops, elbows in the air, never using a napkin, bread lying on the table ... food everywhere. They need to be house trained! How do I get something started?

You must realize that bringing this topic to the table (so to speak), you are intruding upon the cultural norm for many people.

Good manners are not taught in many families or in the schools. What you see as being crude is probably the only way many people have seen others eat.

Your own preferences are more sophisticated, but who is supposed to make this decision for your co-workers?

Ask your boss or human resources whether a workplace etiquette coach can be hired for a short lesson.

At first, your topic will draw some laughter, but you might point out how these "bad manners" look to outsiders, customers, and suppliers. The way people handle their food can make or break a deal in sales, and it can determine whether a prospective new hire gets the job.

Even if management refuses to admit it, poor table etiquette will also affect promotions and perks where people from outside the company are involved.

Corrective action will take leadership from the top.

A person in a uniform is merely an extension of
another person's will.
[Philip Slater]

The Way They Dress

Management is talking about implementing an office uniform because some of the men and women don't know how to dress in a business environment. I agree that we need some lessons around here, but I'm not crazy about a dress code or uniforms. The office is buzzing with rumors, but I wonder whether I should talk to the boss about bringing in an expert to teach some classes before going to a uniform.

Many corporations have standardized dress codes to establish the "image" that is important to success.

Some of the dress codes specify the exact type of clothing; others are more general in what they require.

If your company needs the dress codes because some employees just don't know how to dress for the corporate environment, an outside trainer and coach could help overcome the hard feelings that will arise when the new rules are announced.

Keep in mind that America has seen a considerable shift in what is acceptable for various occasions. The workplace adopted "casual Friday" at the request of workers, and this permission has expanded into everyday being a casual day.

The dressier requirements for dining out, social events, church, and even weddings have come way down from what they were just a few short years ago.

In the end, some people will be unwilling to participate. Decisions will have to be made about the company's expectations and about the continued employment for the refuseniks.

An ounce of loyalty is worth a pound of cleverness.
[Elbert Hubbard]

One Way Loyalty

How can I get my staff to display a little more loyalty to me and the company? They come in late, extend their breaks, and jump out the door right on the clock no matter what work must be done.

Loyalty goes both ways.

The best way to increase loyalty among employees is to demonstrate your own loyalty to them as individuals and your own loyalty to the company.

Your own extra-long work hours and uber-effort do not equate to loyalty to subordinates. You'll have to let them see you supporting them, treating them fairly, and developing their skills if you want them to be loyal to you.

Consider whether you are:

- Providing sufficient feedback about the work being done
- Communicating company successes, failures, and concerns
- Establishing good management-worker rapport
- Building teamwork

Recognition and loyalty go a long way in employee retention, reducing turnover, and boosting productivity.

And successful leaders know that the level of employee loyalty is a leadership responsibility. Take a look at what you can do to improve loyalty toward your entire staff instead of expecting everyone else to change.

By faithfully working eight hours a day, you
may eventually get to be a boss and work
twelve hours a day.
[Robert Frost]

Recognize Achievement

It seems that my boss doesn't know what all I do, and she never compliments my work, no matter how good it is. How can I make sure I'm doing a good job?

This might be a communications problem rather than a recognition problem.

Your boss might never understand the importance of appropriate recognition unless you do something about it.

- Schedule some time to ask for feedback from the boss on what you're doing.

- Make sure the boss knows the scope of your work.

- Set up a system for constant information exchange or feedback.

- Ask how the boss wants to be kept informed: e-mail, memo, short meetings, etc.

- Keep submitting the information and ask for feedback when you want it.

You're probably not the only person feeling this lack of recognition, so any improvement you can bring about will be a bonus for everyone else—including the boss!

Accomplishing the impossible means only the boss
will add it to your regular duties.
[Doug Larson]

My Boss Doesn't Listen to Me

My boss gives instructions, and I can actually see him tune out when I ask questions about what he wants done. How can I hold his attention long enough to make sure I understand what he wants done?

Find out whether you're the only one the boss tunes out. See what others are doing to get attention. Set up a meeting with the boss to discuss just this subject.

Be objective in discussing the issue so you don't wind up in an argument with the boss. Instead of telling the boss he isn't listening, explain that you need a little more attention when he gives instructions. Ask the boss how he wants you to communicate. Does he like ideas in writing or verbal ... maybe email?

The next time he's giving you instructions, decide whether it's a good time to ask your questions. If he's stressed about something else, you'll want to return at a better time to get the information you want.

Establish a time of day or a day a week when you'll update the boss on everything and ask for feedback ... 10 minutes or so max...back up your topics with memos that you can leave behind after you give the highlights.

It's easy to see the amount of stress caused by this lack of communications, so work on the situation until it is resolved. If boss is unwilling to concede on communications, you might have to decide whether this is the best place for you to work.

Life is a series of additions and subtractions.
You control the calculator.
[Gail McMeekin]

Virtual Workplace

All of my work is on a computer, and we could easily transfer data on line so I could work from home. But my boss won't even listen to the idea. How can I get management's attention on this?

Good leaders usually consider the value of each employee suggestion. However, there are occasions where culture is a bigger influence than logic.

If managers earned their rank in a time where everyone worked at a desk under the hawk-eye supervision of the boss, you'll probably find them enforcing the same kind of work environment.

Younger managers who understand the accuracy and capability of 21st century technology are probably more likely to permit remote working.

There might be significant reasons why companies don't want to entertain the idea of off-site work (security of documents, sensitive personal information, etc.), but if there are no good reasons to keep business on site, management should at least consider the possibilities.

A little flexibility here might be a way to keep good employees in today's work environment. As Y-generation managers take over in the future, remote work sites will probably be standard operating procedure.

In the meantime, please remember that the company has been operating like this for a long time. You accepted the conditions with the employment and should not waste energy complaining about established procedures.

To handle yourself, use your head; to
handle others, use your heart.
[Donald Laird]

No Team Spirit

I feel like the Lone Ranger on my job. Plenty of people work near me, but there is no team spirit. Any ideas on how we can improve the teamwork here?

This "working alone" is indicative of disengaged workers. People around you are putting in time and watching the clock instead of being engaged with their work and with others.

Leaders are responsible for these attitudes and for the team spirit that is so important in maximizing productivity and retaining key employees. Any time workers feel they are "working alone," leaders need to implement easy-to-do team building exercises and let everyone feel they are part of the family.

For a quick fix, your company could consider hiring a professional team-building expert to visit your site and conduct training. This also works well for company-wide experiences.

If the team you're speaking of is just a few people or small management team, you'll want to consider an off-site teambuilding exercise. Again, you can hire an expert to join you at a resort or at another suitable place. There are also permanent sites that your team can visit to rejuvenate your team spirit.

It is very important that your top management get involved, maybe with training of their own, to help them understand their role in building and maintaining team spirit. Good team spirit increases productivity and profits. Money spent building team spirit is an investment.

I want to get a tattoo of myself on my entire
body, only two inches taller.
[Steven Wright]

Tattoos and Piercings

Our boss just told us we'll have to cover our tattoos and piercings while at work. This body art cost a lot of money, and I want to show it off. Is it smart for the boss to make this kind of policy?

Let's assume that the tattoos and piercings you're talking about are either on your head, neck, or arms (because if you're talking about other places where your artwork shows, a different comment is needed)!

Basically, the policy depends on the effect of this art on the business. If customers find it attractive, the boss might want to encourage display of the art and even hire people who are willing to get tattoos and piercings. On the other hand, if the art has a negative effect on business, the boss might ask that you cover it.

Tattoos and piercings are not protected by the same laws that require equality in race, creed, color, sex, and disabilities. What we're talking about here is pretty much like a dress code—accept it or move along.

Now, if you're working "in the back" where you don't come into contact with customers, the boss really should consider the advisability of such a policy. Your company might miss out on the talent and skills of some excellent people if they judge the person's suitability on whether they display their body art.

Your action depends on whether you want to keep your job.

Good tattoos aren't cheap and cheap
tattoos aren't good.
[Anonymous]

More on Tattoos

My boy friend bought me a great tattoo for Christmas, but my company just announced that this tattoo won't be permissible under the new dress code effective next month. The tattoo is high on the back of my neck, so I can't very well hide it all the time. Can the company really forbid body art?

Studies show that most tattoos and piercings are acquired before age 24, before people understand what these body modifications might mean for their corporate advancement.

Management's attitude toward tattoos and piercings might change as a younger crowd moves into leadership, but for now, visible body art won't help you advance.

About 1/3 of companies address tattoos and piercings in their dress codes. Other businesses have a policy for employees who are in face-to-face contact with customers—the "cover 'em up" or "find-a-new-job policy."

Corporate policies about tattoos and piercings have been challenged unsuccessfully in court, so the short answer to your question is that the company can forbid display of both tattoos and piercings. The question you might want to ask, however, is not whether the policies can be enforced but whether your appearance will have an affect on your success.

Do people in top management have tattoos and piercings that show? Are other people with body art getting pay raises and promotions? Or, are these good things going to people who comply with the policy your company will soon announce?

Good things happen when you pay attention.
[John F. Smith]

Boss Continues Paper Work When I'm Speaking

When I go into my boss' office, he speaks to me, but he continues to read the papers on his desk while I talk. How do I get his attention?

This is a real problem. It could mean that the guy doesn't care about you at all, or it could mean that he just doesn't know any better.

Some bosses act this way because they are just rude people. Some others are just so stressed that they are trying to multi-task.

I found that I was doing the same kind of thing when I continued to keyboard my work while listening to my assistant.

In my case, I did look up at him, but he finally told me that it was too weird for me to type while talking with him. If he hadn't told me how much it bothered him, I wouldn't have had a clue.

So here's the solution. If your boss recognizes your presence but doesn't look at you while you talk, just stop talking until he does look up.

Resume your presentation when he looks at you, but stop again if he looks away. If you stop talking, he'll look up, for sure.

If he tries to get you to talk while he works on other matters, tell him the same thing my assistant said to me, "This is too weird, I'll be back when you're not so busy."

Limburger is also fermented with Brevibacterium, the same bacteria responsible for body odor, and this contributes to the odor.
[Unclestinky.wordpress.com]

Popcorn and Stinky Lunches

Some people stink up our office everyday. One of them makes microwave popcorn for a morning snack. Another microwaves some kind of stinking lunch everyday (smells as bad as limburger cheese), and the third nukes popcorn in the afternoon. Twenty people work here, and the rest of us have tried to tolerate these noxious aromas. But I'm getting to the end of my rope. How can I get them to stop stinking up the place?

Let's assume that you've already asked them if they could prepare some alternative that doesn't have such a strong aroma—because that's the first thing to try.

I have to agree that some microwave popcorns have a more agreeable aroma than others. Some smell as good as fresh popped corn. Some brands are just as strong in the other direction.

And limburger cheese aroma ... whew! I'm told that the only people who don't find the odor repelling are those who are actually eating the stuff.

If these three people are unwilling to change their diet a little upon the request of everyone else, the boss might have to get involved. Well, unless the boss is one of the offenders!

If the friendly approach doesn't work, the boss can explain the facts of life to these smelly people or get rid of the microwave.

I'll take fifty percent efficiency to get
one hundred percent loyalty.
[Samuel Goldwyn]

Company Loyalty

My people don't give a hoot about the company. We have better perks and salary than others around here, but we just can't get people interested in doing their best or in helping grow the company. Ideas?

You've probably heard before that employee loyalty is the responsibility of leadership and that loyalty among workers is affected by the quality of leadership in the company.

Here are three things needed to improve employee loyalty:

1. Meet regularly with employees. If you can't meet with the entire company, meet with your direct reports and have each department or section meet frequently enough so everyone knows what's going on.

2. Ask opinions. Get input from front line employees before decisions are announced. Get their feedback on plans and on current activities. You'll find important ideas that will affect implementation of your plans.

3. Tell all about it. Let employees know everything you can about your company: finances, sales goals, manufacturing achievements, problems, and employee situations. They hear the rumors; now let them know the facts.

It might be a good idea for you to participate in a leadership seminar or arrange for some in-depth leadership coaching. There are plenty of experts who can help tune up your leadership skills, but if you refuse to accept responsibility for poor company loyalty, you won't get anywhere.

The only way to compete for these top candidates
is to give them flexibility to go back to school
or to pursue outside activities, or to find a way to
supplement their income.
[Matt Dornic]

Flex Schedules

I like my company, but I've been offered a job where I would get more time off and have some flexibility in my schedule. My boss hasn't been flexible at all, and I wonder whether I should push for a better schedule here or just go with the new company.

There might be some reasons why your company cannot allow flexible schedules, but your boss needs to pay attention.

A recent survey showed that 41% of companies have increased the number of days off and 36% now allow alternative work arrangements such as flex schedules or working from home.

You know how important this is to you, but your boss sees it as an "exception to the rule." The boss is concerned that if you're allowed to have flextime, everyone in the company will want the same opportunity.

The boss might trust *you*, but can everyone be trusted with this type of schedule?

Meet with your boss and explain that you'd like to stay with the company, but this is important to you. Ask what the company can do.

Give management some time to get back with you. Then make your decision about staying or leaving.

Finally, be sure you have an alternative before you bring up this subject with the boss. You might very well be told to pack up and move along if your request appears to management as an ultimatum.

Never be the first to arrive at a party or the last to go home and never, never be both.
[David Brown]

Office Parties

What can I do about the office party that I don't want to go to? My boss announced that attendance is mandatory. The party is after work hours at a restaurant across town. Everybody always gets drunk and it's embarrassing. Do I have to go?

This type party and your personal beliefs put you in an awkward position. Basically, you are being told to do something with which you don't want to be associated.

Here's the thing. Only go to the party if you want to protect your success in the company:

- Set the schedule ahead of time, saying beforehand that you can only stay for about an hour

- At the party, visit with key people right away— before they get to the forgetful zone. They'll remember that you attended, and they'll remember that you left before they embarrassed themselves.

- Leave as you have scheduled. Make the rounds the next day and thank the bosses for a great office party.

- You'll stand out if you send a hand-written thank-you note through the mail (not interoffice distribution) in addition to the verbal acknowledgment.

- Everyone will admire you for finding the middle ground—unless you brag about your strategy. So keep your plans to yourself.

If a man fools you once, he's a jerk. If he fools
you twice, you're a jerk."
[Anonymous]

My Boss is A Jerk

My boss is a jerk, and I wonder what I should do to protect myself. This guy doesn't keep his promises or give anyone else recognition. Sometimes he gives us the silent treatment, and other times he talks about employees with other people who work here. Since bosses come and go, I'm wondering whether to just put up with it or to make it an issue.

Here's what you should do.

1. Don't get angry, and don't stress over this.

2. Don't get in a fight with the boss.

3. Keep your good reputation in the company.

4. Do more than is expected.

5. Decide which is more important, this job or moving elsewhere.

Even if others have been silent about this, you're not the only one who knows this guy is a jerk. This person is making a contribution of some kind that makes it worthwhile to keep him on the staff. Since the higher-ups value his presence for some reason, you need to make your decision about whether you want to stay with this company.

Remain silent about the problem. Other employees will raise the issue, and you'll see how things play out. If you're leaving, dust off that resume and get busy. Either way, you'll be better off just taking care of business.

Adults can take a simple holiday for children and screw it up. What began as a presentation of simple gifts to delight and surprise children around the Christmas tree has culminated in a woman opening up six shrimp forks from her dog, who drew her name.
[Erma Bombeck]

Christmas Gifts at Work

I hate having to find gifts for my employees at Christmas time. Meaningful gifts cost too much, and the junk gifts most people give wind up collecting dust until they're thrown away. Is there some way I can get out of this meaningless cycle of giving stuff people don't want?

In spite of the million dollar bonuses that high rollers are seeing at the end of the year, surveys show that the number of companies giving gifts is dropping rapidly.

Some companies are caught up in a general gift exchange where people draw names and play a game with the giving (and taking back) of gifts. Other companies simply permit a holiday exchange of gifts among employees if they wish to do so. And in many companies, managers buy a small gift for each employee.

Surveys show that 75% of employees prefer a gift card, and a lot of offices are opting out of individual gifts and buying something for the office that everyone can enjoy (new microwave for the break room, etc).

When bosses give actual gifts instead of bonuses, they often find that some employees feel obligated to return the favor. That's when bosses realize just how much junk there is in the gift department.

If you have a diverse workforce, you'll find that a number of people just don't recognize this as a time of year for gift giving with some people refusing to accept such gifts. If you dislike giving gifts, now is a good time to announce that you're discontinuing the practice and, for example, giving employees an extra half-day off instead.

The only risk of failure is promotion.
[Scott Adams]

Passed Over

For fifteen years my workplace evaluations have been top notch, but a newly-hired young MBA was just promoted over me. I'm steamed, but I don't know how big a deal I should make of this with management. Any advice?

Whatever you do, make sure you don't have a heated argument with your boss about this promotion.

It's ok to have a conversation to find out what happened, but you can be sure that management is aware of your tenure, and they are aware of the young MBA's experience level.

A lot goes into these decisions that is usually not revealed to interested parties, things such as whether the company is being positioned for sale, whether the promotion is part of a grooming/training process, or whether management sees something in the promoted person's qualities that they don't see in that of the passed over individual.

You've been there fifteen years; management knows you well. They remember occasions when you have met expectations and when you haven't.

So, talk it over with the boss, but don't expect a change in the promotion. This is something you'll have to accept (and act happy about) or go to work for someone else. You'll be the loser if you bicker about it with management or with other employees.

If your work attitude isn't happy and helpful, your new boss will make sure your tenure with this company is cut short.

Extroverts seem to be more accepting of
lengthy eye contact.
[Dale Collie]

Eye Contact vs. Staring

There's this guy in my office who stares too intently when we're in conversation. His eyes are piercing, and he makes almost everyone uncomfortable. We don't know whether he does this to dominate the conversation or whether he is unaware of how he comes across. He's a good guy and contributes to the team effort, but we're all starting to avoid him. Any ideas on how to handle the situation?

Let's start by assuming that this staring guy is unaware of what he's doing. He might just think he's being polite and listening carefully.

His culture might see this kind of piercing look as a compliment to the speaker. Even if he comes from the same area as you do, his family culture could be significantly different from what you're used to.

Many people have certain minor body language habits that might turn off other people. Some people stand too close in conversation. Some pick their noses. Others crack their knuckles or make other bodily noises!

A good friend, or at least a business friend, should have a conversation with this guy. A compliment about his listening skills would set up the conversation.

If the guy has an ocular problem, he'll mention it. Otherwise, the friend can explain that in American business culture, three seconds is about the max for eye contact without making the other person nervous. And then go on to offer a tip about his eye contact lasting much longer.

Before alleging misconduct you really should make
sure that the issue is really worth the risk.
[Dale Collie]

Management Violation of Company Policy

Company policy says company cars must never be used for personal business. I don't understand why upper management can get away with using them however they like. A fellow worker saw a VP leaving the dry cleaner a few days ago—in the company car! Should I bring this up to management?

The employee who observed this apparent violation should discuss the topic with his immediate supervisor. It's up to the supervisor to check this out with management.

The VP might have special privileges, or the VP might actually be in violation of the policy. Either way, the company has a problem.

If the VP has special privileges, the policy needs to address these exceptions so everyone understands what's going on. If the VP is in violation, the company can wind up with problems later on when some other employee finds themselves in an accident while they, too, are violating the policy—and pointing the finger at the VP who is a known violator.

It will be tough for the company to "punish" the low-level employee if management is also in violation.

With "minor" infractions such as this, employees observing the apparent violations have done their jobs if they report it to their immediate supervisor. Infractions of consequence might require higher-level exposure. Either way, enforcing violations of company policies is a leadership responsibility.

Be careful of your thoughts; they may become
words at any moment.
[Ira Gassen]

Boss Won't Listen to Good Ideas

Sometimes my boss is a tyrant. Every time I bring up a better way to do my job, he goes ballistic. Is there some way to convince him that our creative front line ideas are worth listening to?

As someone once said, "Even the thinnest sheet of paper has two sides to it." You probably do have a helpful suggestion, but it seems like the boss doesn't see it as being so great.

Here are three ways to look at it:

- Maybe the boss doesn't listen because you don't have good ideas—according to his way of thinking.

- Maybe the boss is insecure and takes no suggestions for fear that they won't meet his expectations.

- Perhaps you don't see the big picture that the boss has for your company.

If you're the only person being ignored, you might work on this through a personal conversation, telling the boss in a conversational tone just how you feel when you are ignored. If you're passionate about the change you're recommending, you might find out how this idea is working elsewhere. Get an outside expert's opinion, and build a written case.

More likely, though, you should forget about the recommendations and focus on the work you were hired to do with the tools the boss gives you. You brought up the idea; the boss didn't like it. Drop it.

Does the advent of the cubicle mean that common
courtesy dies an inglorious death?
[Jason Thomas – BaltimoreMick.com/blog]

Office Etiquette

The first morning on the job, a new hire sat on the boss' desk while being given instructions for the day. While seated on the visitor's side of a co-worker's desk the next day, the novice put his feet on the desk. This morning the "jerk" belched out loud during the staff meeting. How can we housetrain this otherwise capable young person?

As I heard someone say one time, this person hasn't been socialized properly. In spite of the formal education received, they just don't understand the acceptable behavior of working with others.

If you don't do anything, this person will become such an annoyance he will be fired.

If you want to be involved personally, you can have a conversation about how this kind of thing will affect their career; then tackle the abnormal behaviors one by one, explaining the what and why behind each problem you observe. With the proper conversation and explanation, your assistance can turn things around and help this person become a stellar employee.

Another alternative is to send the offender to a business etiquette course.

I hope you don't feel like you must bring in an etiquette coach for everyone just to train this one person, but if everyone is interested in polishing their skills you can consider having an expert present some lunchtime seminars for the whole company.

We can all use some reminders from time to time to stay at the top of our etiquette game.

Vacation: Two weeks on the sunny sands - and the
rest of the year on the financial rocks.
[Sam Ewing]

Vacation Schedules

Our company requires us to schedule our annual vacations almost a year in advance. I don't have a clue as to what I want to do for next year's vacation or when my wife can take her vacation. Is it right for companies to require planning this far ahead?

Vacation schedules can be a real problem in companies where everyone takes off whenever it suits them. It isn't easy for management to meet operating demands or customer needs if they don't know when employees will be away.

Some companies overcome this by shutting down operations for two weeks each year. Others ask employees to request vacation dates a year in advance so they can reschedule some people to keep things going or bring in temps to fill the jobs. It isn't unreasonable for employers to ask.

The problem with spouse vacation schedules is widespread. Your spouse might try to put in a vacation request for the same dates you use, or at least have a conversation with the boss to see if there are any conflicts and whether there is any flexibility if the two of you wind up with different vacation schedules.

Make the best plan you can with what you do know and then try to trade with someone if your actual plans require some other dates.

Doing your own job well is the first step in
being a good team member.
[Dale Collie]

Bad Attitudes

Some people in my office just don't do their jobs the way they should be done. They're late with their projects; some of the information is incorrect, and they have a bad attitude about the company. What should I do about this?

If you're a co-worker, you need to pay attention to your own job. If you were the manager, you'd be responsible for making sure others do their jobs the way they should be done, and you could work on their attitudes.

As it is, you are employed to take care of a specific job; you're not there to monitor others.

Bringing this to the attention of the boss will just get you in trouble with your fellow employees for reporting them and with your bosses for telling them they aren't doing their jobs.

Relax and enjoy your day or look for another job.

If you're the manager, you'd better get on the ball and correct these issues. The problem is probably motivation and leadership vs. individual incompetence. For managers, this is no time to relax.

Too much work and too much energy kill a
man just as effectively as too much assorted
vice or too much drink.
[Rudyard Kipling]

Too Much Work

I have too much work to do. What can I do about it?

1. List your tasks and responsibilities.

2. Establish priorities.

3. Set up a schedule to work on each task.

4. Decide what you can get other people to do.

5. Strategize ways to delegate whatever can be done by others (even if they don't work for you).

6. Eliminate the low priority or unnecessary tasks that are never checked on.

7. Establish a routine for working on the tasks so you have a system.

8. Eliminate redundant tasks.

9. Get the proper training to make you more efficient.

10. Get the proper equipment to do the job correctly.

11. Categorize non-productive activities and eliminate all possible.

Worthwhile goals are those that carry some risk
and seem a little scary!
[Dale Collie]

Individual Goals

My boss always starts off the year talking about individual goals. I can't stand it. I'm going to do my job, and I don't need any goals. Help?

Your company probably requires all direct reports to establish individual goals.

Don't lose any sleep over this, and don't worry about the fact that your job is routine and repetitive.

Consider goals that focus on improving some aspect of your job, such as improving the inbound information that you work with and how you handle it.

You can consider improving your outbound product or the flow of information.

Another way to look at this is to establish goals for self-improvement—performance, education, attitude.

Basically, help your boss by developing goals for your job instead of fighting the system. You'll come out way ahead if you take advantage of the opportunity.

My success, part of it certainly, is that I have
focused in on a few things.
[Bill Gates]

Boss is Scatterbrained

My boss jumps from project to project, and we never know which action should get priority. This morning he told us to give highest priority to a corporate project, and just after lunch he said an in-house project would get priority—after we spent 4 hours on the corporate project. How do we get him focused so we can do our job properly?

Someone who has a good relationship with your boss needs to have a conversation on this topic to explain how his erratic behavior has a negative impact on performance.

Let him know that everyone supports him and wants to make him a big success and that you can do an even better job if he coordinates with you about what needs to be done.

If the conversation is impossible or if it doesn't change anything, you need to just go with his changing demands.

Your responsibility is to do the work given to you. Setting the direction or giving priority is not your challenge. Don't get stressed over these changes in priorities.

I've long thought the "Reply to All" feature of Outlook is one of its most pernicious jokes: it must be intended as a trap for the unwary, the unwise, or the inebriated.

[Cynthia Rowland - WomenLawyerLeaders.blogspot.com]

Email Etiquette

Are some people too dense to observe that they're the only ones typing mile-long emails with no paragraph breaks or that no one else types in all caps? I've explained it to both of these people, but they keep on doing it.

It seems like these people send weird emails because they know it bothers you.

There are several other items of email etiquette that could be taught to people throughout the realm. There are some good books as well as on-line and in-person seminars that can help all of us do a better job writing and handling emails.

But back to your specific case: unless the offender is your boss, you can politely and objectively comment on the format again, saying that it's just so lengthy that you won't be reading their email until they change.

Their action seems to be intentional. You've explained the principles involved. They understand what other people expect.

Don't get angry during this conversation, and don't argue with them. Just make the statement and leave it alone.

Then hit delete every time you see that they've sent something in this "attention getting" format.

That should be easy enough. Right?

Fame lost its appeal for me when I went into a public restroom and an autograph seeker handed me a pen and paper under the stall door.
[Marlo Thomas]

Dirty Restrooms

What can we do about the terrible condition of our restrooms at work? People are very good about keeping the paper towels picked up, but these restrooms never get a good cleaning. They look bad, and they smell bad. It's embarrassing to allow business guests in there.

Someone needs to discuss this with management and the people responsible for cleaning the place.

If the people responsible for keeping the restroom clean don't respond, it might be time for some classes on what is expected, or it might be time to assign some new responsibilities.

This is a matter of hygiene more than appearances. If management can't straighten out the problem, it might be time to seek out a new job. The cleanliness of the restrooms is a reflection of management's concern for the business and for the employees.

It's ok to stand out from the crowd, just make sure you'll look great when the spotlight is on you.
[Dale Collie]

Crazy Cube Décor

Why do people think they can decorate their workspace with weird stuff? They don't do this at home, but they think goofy pictures, posters of sexy people, and noisemakers are just the thing for their space at work. Is there some polite way to tell them this is not your teenager's bedroom?

One more time – are you the boss or a co-worker? If you're the boss, you can announce any policy you like about the way work cubes are decorated.

If you're not the boss, you really need to focus on your own desk top and get your work done.

A lot of companies allow employees to decorate cubes to the extreme, thinking that this freedom makes people feel appreciated, welcomed, and included, no matter how traditional or how bizarre their decorating ideas.

Other companies go back to the idea that only business related items should be displayed at the office.

It seems that your company has opted for the more contemporary approach and has encouraged individual decorating choices.

Save your energy and your sanity. Don't waste any more time complaining about this to the boss or to others. You'll be the loser unless your job description includes monitoring the cube décor of others.

Stress is nothing more than a socially acceptable
form of mental illness.
[Richard Carlson]

Wrong Word

One of my team members frequently uses words by mistake. Whenever I ask what he intended to say, it is as though he never even realized he used the wrong word. Examples—He often refers to other team members or customers by the wrong name or says things like, "When we get together next year ..." when he means to say next week. These are small incidents, but I'm worried about him. Any ideas?

Correct him every time he makes such an error and make a note to yourself so you can establish the frequency.

When you have a few examples, have a discussion with him. Explain the importance of this to the day-to-day operations and let him know this is a sign of extreme workplace stress.

If something isn't done to control the stress, the errors will worsen, and eventually, his health will deteriorate.

He is probably already suffering from lowered immune system or other health issues. Corrective action can help him avoid the health problems as well as mistakes, errors, and accidents that can affect the bottom line.

In addition, your advice will also help make him more popular with those who have started to sense his decline.

The world will not end if you miss a call.
[Dale Collie]

Cell Phones and Interruptions

My boss seems compelled to check his cell phone every time it rings (or vibrates)! It's aggravating to have him tell me to continue with my report while he reads his text message or listens to voice mail. Is there some way I can tell him to pay attention?

Your boss seems addicted to his gadgets. He should pay attention to the live report, the person in his presence, instead of the messages.

You could politely explain that you'll return when his schedule permits your conversation. He'll probably say that he is listening to you and that he can multi-task, but you'll need to advise him that his actions are kind of nerve wracking.

Your best tactic is probably to stop talking when he looks at his cell phone. Don't resume until he looks back at you.

Maybe you can make a joke of it each time you come in for a report, asking him to turn off the cell phone just as speakers ask audience members to silence the ringing of their mobile phones.

Just because nobody complains doesn't mean all
parachutes are perfect.
[Benny Hill]

Griping About the Job

We have a close-knit team where I work, and a new guy was hired a few months ago to replace a retiring co-worker. This guy complains all the time about the job and management. None of us agree with him, but he just won't quit complaining. What can we do to get him on board so he doesn't affect the attitude of everyone here?

You or one of your fellow employees needs to have lunch with this "complainer" and explain in a very casual, non-threatening way that everyone else at the place is happy.

You need to help him understand that no one agrees with him, and that his constant complaining is taking the fun out of the office.

Maybe you could actually tell him that he needs to think about a change—in the way he acts or in where he works.

If he truly doesn't like it at your organization, he should find another place of employment. If the complaining is just a habit or a part of his culture, he needs to know that it isn't winning him any points with the home team.

Since office politics are only fun for insiders, you have
to wonder whether you'll always be on the inside.
[Dale Collie]

Politics in the Office

We have this guy in our office who is very opinionated about who should get our vote in the upcoming election. Everyone else is basically for the other person, but he just won't stop talking about it. Any ideas on how to get him to shut up?

Someone who has a good relationship with the loud mouth should let him know that he is alienating everyone.

If he continues, a couple of people should discuss it with him in a non threatening, helpful way, just so he gets the idea that the issue involves more than just one person's observation.

Be sure to explain that he has every right to make these statements and that no one objects to his holding his point of view. The problem is not what he believes but the way he harangues everyone with his opinions.

Then if he can't control the campaigning, the boss should let him know that bothering everyone isn't going to help his cause and that he should relax on this subject—that if he can't lay off, he might be laid off himself for creating an uncooperative and disruptive workplace.

We know what a person thinks not when he tells
us what he thinks, but by his actions.
[Isaac Bashevis Singer]

Volatile Personality

One guy in our office is so volatile that we just try to avoid him. Sometimes he is totally charming, but sometimes he starts yelling at you just for saying good morning. Is there some way we can get him to be more consistent so we don't always have to walk on egg shells around him?

It might be easier for this guy to be consistent if you want the "screamer" personality all the time.

There is probably some kind of extreme stressor going on in this person's life that creates the ups and downs in his attitudes, but that doesn't make it any easier to deal with him.

Try having a conversation with this tyrant about what else he is struggling with. Maybe you and fellow employees can become a support team regarding the problem area.

At least you can let this guy know that much better support is available from everyone if the "nice voice" is used more consistently.

Every improvement in communication
makes boring people more terrible.
[Frank Moore Colby]

Over-Communicator

My boss is an over-communicator. He over-explains and he over-supervises. Every day he sends me 20-30 email questions about projects I have in the works. How can I get him to back off?

Managers and leaders need to understand that oversight is good, but meddling is out of line.

Have a conversation with your boss about how you feel. Make it very objective by discussing the amount of communication without attacking him.

He might tell you that the "over communication" is required because you consistently misunderstand his instructions and the numerous questions are the result of his lack of confidence in you.

On the other hand, this type of manager usually over-communicates instructions because they lack confidence in their own ability to give instructions.

Suggest that the boss write out the instructions for key projects to make sure you're both on track; better yet, you write out the instructions as you understand them and ask for the boss' approval of your memo.

If the questions continue, suggest that you give your boss a daily update (before lunch or around 4:00 p.m.). Find out how the boss would like for you to communicate the update—verbal, memo, or email. This will give both of you some "breathing room" and provide the feedback to make sure you both know what is expected.

No man goes before his time –
unless the boss leaves early.
[Groucho Marx]

Supervisor Bugs Me

Our new district manager is a real stickler for details and seems to be looking over my shoulder all the time. We both have many years in our jobs, so it's not like I need constant supervision. Is there some way for me to get him off my back?

Yes. You can get him off your back by doing everything he asks. He's the boss. He has his own style of management.

Let's admire his interest because complaining about him or his style will be a waste of energy, and it might cost you your job.

To build a high degree of comfort for the new manager, consider the following:

1. Do everything the manager asks. Do a better job than he expects. Do more than he expects.

2. Make a note of everything you discuss so you don't overlook anything. The one thing you fail to do is the one thing he will check.

3. Keep the manager informed frequently and in the way he or she prefers, e.g. email, voice mail, phone calls, in person, etc.

This type of manager has a very high need for hands-on managing and results. Keep the manager comfortable by embracing his guidance enthusiastically and by keeping him informed.

Pretty soon, you'll be the proverbial "golden store manager," and the boss will let up on his detailed approach.

Police in Radnor, Pennsylvania, interrogated a suspect by placing a metal colander on his head and connecting it with wires to a photocopy machine. The message "He's lying" was placed in the copier, and police pressed the copy button each time they thought the suspect wasn't telling the truth. Believing the "lie detector" was working, the suspect confessed.
[Urban Legend – Fiction]

Office Responsibilities

Our copy machine is out of paper almost every time I go to use it. What can we do to get people to put in paper when they know it's empty?

1. Paper in the copy machine is a management responsibility. The boss should develop and enforce policies about who is responsible for routine office tasks.

2. There should be an office policy that says a certain person is responsible for stocking paper at certain times during the day. The frequency would depend on how much usage the machine gets.

3. A trained, designated person filling the machine decreases the opportunity for failure and maintenance costs.

4. If you have a small office, work out an agreement as to who checks the paper, orders supplies, and calls maintenance.

5. If you're in a large office, see if the boss will accept a recommendation on how these tasks should be accomplished.

Even if you figure out what the politics game is . . . the worst thing you can do is avoid it. It will catch up to you, and it will bite you in the rear.
[Marilyn Puder-York]

Office Politics

The people who get ahead where I work are the same people who schmooze management, buy their lunches, bring small gifts, start damaging rumors, and laugh the loudest at the non-funny jokes. As a manager myself, how can I help break this cycle of rewarding only the "brown nosers?"

Office politics is one of the most common workplace stressors and costs companies a lot of money.

Leaders are responsible for controlling these issues. Here are some proven tactics to use in correcting this situation:

1. Publicly disapprove of blatant office politics whenever you detect it.

2. Give special attention to those who actually achieve instead of those who try to grab the glory for projects and ideas away from those who deserve credit.

3. Reward managers who credit subordinates instead of taking credit for themselves.

4. Discipline those managers who fail to give credit where it is due.

5. Address rumors and half-truths on the spot and follow up with another form of communication about the issue, e.g. correct the rumor verbally when you hear it and then send a memo to everyone about what you heard along with the facts.

The 60s are gone, dope will never be as cheap, sex never as free, and the rock and roll never as great.
[Abbie Hoffman]

Music Style

I'm in my 50's, and the 20 year old guy who shares the office plays music that's driving me crazy. How can I convince him that this rock stuff isn't suitable for the workplace?

This isn't the first generation to be upset by the music of younger people. Trying to convince them to enjoy your music is about as tough as getting you to tune to their station.

Relax about this and find another way to tune in to your own tunes.

Maybe you can come to an agreement about which time of day you'll play your music and when the other guy can play his.

You might have to both get headsets that give you the music and still permit conversation and telephone calls.

Of course, you'll have to learn how to operate an iPod or some other mp3 device ... a change will be good for you.

On second thought, a change of music might be good for both of you. Look for some middle ground in music styles. Until you reach some agreement on all of this or find a technology that works for both of you, you should probably just concede the choice of music to the younger employee.

If you don't, you're going to lose the sharp "youngsters" and their valuable input—and their replacement will just as likely enjoy some kind of music you don't like.

There's nothing like eavesdropping to show you that
the world outside your head is different from the
world inside your head.
[Thornton Wilder]

Eavesdropping

When I'm on the phone with customers, people in the office cubes near me often laugh at funny things I say or add their own remarks. It's all clean fun, but very distracting. How can I get them to pay attention to their own work and leave me alone while I'm on the phone?

It's impossible to get the voyeurs to keep their distance. Get a headset that covers your ears and works with your telephone to block out all of the ambient noise.

Maybe you can find something that works with your iPod so you can listen to music when you're not on the phone.

This type of equipment blocks out the wisecracks and gives you an excuse for not responding to all of those unwanted remarks.

A joke is a very serious thing.
[Winston Churchill]

Joking Around

Too many of our employees think the office is a place to joke around. Other than a crackdown by upper management, is there anything we can do to limit the amount of laughter and wisecracks? I'm falling behind in my work.

It's too bad that you're having a hard time with the "fun at work."

Most companies are trying to lighten up and have a little fun, but all this laughter seems to be getting in your way.

People require different circumstances to get their best work done. Some need the silence of a tomb, and others require the high energy of Starbucks.

If your Type A genes require more structure, try allotting yourself a small amount of time to really appreciate the friendship and joy, then focus on your work.

Maybe you can move into the conference room when you have a project that requires your full attention. Perhaps you can take some of your work to the public library. With a little practice, you can concentrate in the midst of everyone else's levity.

Do not "report" this situation to your boss. Chances are good that the boss is already aware of it, and there's a good chance that the boss has encouraged this environment.

Most people work just hard enough not to get fired
and get paid just enough money not to quit.
[George Carlin]

Everyone's Leaving

My boss doesn't have a clue that half the people in our office are looking for a new job. Should someone tell him or let him suffer the consequences of poor leadership? I'm worried about all the extra work this is going to mean for me if I stay here when others are jumping ship.

This is another situation where there is little advantage in reporting the facts to your boss.

These "leavers" might not really be on the way out. They might just be talking about it or joining the conversation to see what it sounds like when they say these things aloud. They sure won't appreciate your telling the boss that they have plans to exit.

If they really are planning to leave and you're planning to stay, you need to position yourself to take advantage of their departure. Stay out of their conversations. You don't want one of them telling the boss that *you* are taking flight. Do your job to the best of your ability. Learn how to do the job of someone whose position appeals to you. If they leave, you might be able to capture their job.

And quit worrying about the amount of work that evolves if all of them leave. They won't all leave at the same time. Some of them will never leave. And the work you do during a day is just that—a day's work. Don't stress about what isn't getting done. That's the boss' problem. Just do your own work and leave the worries behind as you go out the door.

Until you are promoted to a position of hiring and firing, this isn't your problem.

Eating rice cakes is like chewing on a foam
coffee cup, only less filling.
[Dave Berry]

Break Room

Our boss just announced that our break room is going to start using 100% disposable cups, plates, and utensils—no more coffee mugs, soup bowls, forks or knives—all plastic and paper. Sanitation is the reason for the change, but many of us just don't like drinking coffee from paper cups. What should we do?

Relax a little. Just bring your own insulated mug from Starbucks and keep it at your desk.

It seems like the boss is concerned about the pile of dirty cups, plates, and silverware left in the break room sink. No one wants to clean up after the break, so get on the bandwagon with the paper and plastic.

Your boss isn't going to complain about your carrying around a cool mug that has a lid on it—especially if you wash it and put it in your desk drawer when you're not using it.

The reward for work well done is the
opportunity to do more.
[Jonas Salk]

Who's Fooling Whom?

We have a couple of people who are always at work. They come in before everyone else and when everyone else is going home, they make a fresh pot of coffee. Are these people showing off or is all this extra time required to get their work done?

There are several reasons why someone would spend a lot of "extra" time at the office.

- The workload might require their presence.

- Their work might be an escape from something at home.

- Perhaps they lose all of their daytime productivity through meetings and interruptions and wind up staying late to get their basic work completed.

- Or it could be as suggested, that they are just trying to get brownie points from the boss by putting in extra time.

Management might like the idea of someone working so much, but they should really take a look and see if it is required. There might be short-term gains for the company, but if it goes on for some time, there is a good chance that the person will burn out and leave or at the minimum, become less efficient and productive during the regular work hours.

No need to complain to anyone about their actions. Just do your own work and be happy that you can get out of there on time. No one is comparing your time on the clock with anyone else–unless you're abusing the system, of course.

In war, there are no unwounded soldiers.
[José Narosky]

Special Treatment

Every Veterans Day our company does something special for veterans. Last year, they had the day off. This year it was a free lunch at an expensive place. This seems unfair to the rest of us. How can we get in on the benefits?

You can get these benefits by joining the US Army, Navy, Air Force, Marines, or Coast Guard.

That's it!

It doesn't make a difference what temperature a room is, it's always room temperature."
[Stephen Wright]

Too Hot – Too Cold

It's way too cold at my desk, and across the room, it is way too hot for others working there. Our boss tells me to put on another sweater, and he tells the others to open a window. How can we convince the boss to get furnace repair out here and correct this problem?

The boss needs to understand that his cavalier approach is costing him money—lots of it.

In addition to the heat lost through open windows, he's losing productivity by the hour. Physical discomfort is a primary workplace stressor and contributes to significantly reduced productivity.

Even if he doesn't care about the comfort of employees, he should be held accountable for costs— both heating costs and productivity.

Have an objective, light-hearted discussion with him about this and ask for approval to call the heating repair people. If the response is negative, ask for permission to use a space heater near your desk (check to make sure it is safe to do so).

If you cannot get warm, think about whether this is the right place for you to spend your work days.

You cannot kill time without injuring eternity.
[Henry David Thoreau]

Show up On Time

How can I get people to show up on time for our meetings? Every latecomer has a good excuse, but tardiness interrupts the meeting and causes us to review what has been covered already. Any ideas?

Leaders can use various threats and demands to get people to show up on time, but leading people in a way that makes them want to show up on time is much more effective.

Make sure the agenda is distributed before the meeting and that everyone present will have some responsibility.

Instead of having each person give a routine report, ask them to reveal a particular challenge they are facing and allow everyone else to brainstorm ways to solve the problem.

Schedule meetings for appropriate times and days, not when you're trying to control workplace attendance (e.g. Friday afternoon).

Management is responsible for conducting meaningful meetings that people want to attend. If people are skipping your meeting or showing up late, there's a message in it for you.

Now, if you just want to badger people into showing up on time, close and lock the door at the exact time the meeting is to begin. Don't let the latecomers in. They'll get the message and be on time for the next meeting.

The average American worker has fifty
interruptions a day, of which seventy percent
have nothing to do with work.
[W. Edwards Deming]

Workplace Interruptions

I can't work 10 minutes without somebody walking in my office or ringing my phone. Is there some way to keep people from interrupting my work all day long?

1. Schedule Time—Establish a pattern for your work. Decide ahead of time when you'll check email and voice mail and when you'll do various tasks.

2. Establish Procedures—Establish procedures so everyone knows what is expected and how to complete the task. You shouldn't be giving directions for every task that develops.

3. Delegate Authority Along With Responsibility—Train people to do the job and give them authority to do what needs to be done. Don't let them delegate the decisions back up to you.

4. Train People to Make Their Own Decisions—Allow people to make decisions even if their methods differ from what you would choose. If they are capable employees, they'll get the job done. If they are not capable, you have a different problem.

5. Schedule time for Personal Interaction—Be sure employees have time to give and get feedback. If you schedule the time, they won't interrupt you when you're trying to complete other work.

Three may keep a secret if two of them are dead.
[Benjamin Franklin]

Can You Keep a Secret?

A workplace friend just told me in the greatest confidence that she has accepted a new job offer, but she's not going to give the company any notice. Our company will suffer a huge set back on an important project if this happens, and my own job will be in jeopardy. Should I tell management what I know even though I've been sworn to secrecy?

Go tell your boss now. You can let the boss know that you were asked to keep this secret, but you owe it to your company and yourself to allow enough time to get a replacement.

Now, there is a chance that the person did not actually accept another job. She might be testing your loyalty to see whether you will reveal the *secret*. However, you cannot risk your own job or the company's profits because of some "loyalty" that you do not have.

The request for confidentiality is unfair and unethical of your "friend." Most people are aware of the damage caused by not giving notice of their impending departure. If your friend is leaving, revealing the information will be beneficial to you and the company. If your friend is not leaving, you don't want this friendship anyway.

Clever bosses can prepare for the departure of employees, even if they have not officially "given notice" of their plans. If you want to be a loyal employee, you'll go see the boss right away.

Work will fill the time available for its completion.
[Parkinson's Law]

Get More Work Done

My employees could get more work done if they didn't spend so much time interrupting each other. How can I get people to pay more attention to their work and less attention to gossiping and ball game results?

The chat time is important for your office. The socializing creates a more relaxed work environment and could contribute to increased productivity. If you find that workplace stress is high in spite of the socializing, you might discover that your team is suffering from one of the top ten stressors—not enough work!

Evaluate the workload. Make sure the work is evenly distributed. Then decide whether you have too many people or whether you should add more work.

If your assessment shows that the workload is appropriate and evenly distributed with room for more, you can start adding projects slowly, with deadlines. Make sure the projects are actually needed and that the deadlines are reasonable, then keep adding work until everyone is focused on getting the job done.

You could also try establishing blocks of time where no one in the office communicates with each other by phone, email or in person. Designate specific times when they'll coordinate with each other. Add some break times for socializing. Discuss the whole thing in a positive way, such as "I'd like to help you cut down on interruptions but still have time to talk with friends at the office." Avoid approaching the subject by announcing, "You're not getting your work done."

When I got out of high school they retired my jersey,
but it was for hygiene and sanitary reasons
[George Carlin]

Personal Hygiene

The guy who shares my cubicle frequently clips his fingernails at his desk—clip, clip, clip—nails going everywhere. I've mentioned that the office is not the place for personal hygiene, but he just laughs and keeps on clipping. Is there some way we can discourage this rude behavior?

This unprofessional behavior is either a result of inadequate training or an intentional effort to be rude.

Chances are slim that you'll convince him to change his ways. And if you ask management to order him to stop, he'll find another way to bug you. You'll be even more of a target if you try to change his behavior by doing things that bother him. A regular feud could erupt!

Some companies change behavior by conducting lunchtime presentations about hygiene, manners, and other practices that are part of polite society.

Presentations such as these are effective if the trainer/speaker has a good sense of humor and understands how to interact with the audience. Because they don't work with these people every day as you do, professional speakers can get away with telling people things that are kind of embarrassing for you to talk about . Maybe you can:

1. Bring in a series of lunchtime speakers/trainers
2. Include articles about hygiene and manners in the company newsletter
3. Buy the guy a manicure gift certificate

Work as though you would live forever, and live as though you would die today.
[Og Mandino]

Do Your Own Job

Our company is developing some truly stupid commercials. My job doesn't involve me directly with these commercials, but I hate to see the company going in the wrong direction. Should I say something about all of this to management?

OK, here's the short answer ... keep your mouth shut and do your own job.

You were not hired to oversee corporate advertising, and your "uninformed" opinion will not be welcomed by the CEO or by the "experts" in advertising.

There's a trend toward "stupid" commercials, and there are many things that influence the style of advertising.

If you are worried about the future of the company, you're free to look for employment elsewhere. In the meantime, you'll be much happier if you focus on what you were hired to do.

By the way, make sure you're doing your best and not losing energy by complaining about another department or other employees who are also trying to do their best.

Gambling: The sure way of getting
nothing from something.
[Wilson Mizner]

Betting on Sports Games

I don't know a thing about sports, but our office is consumed with who will win the big football game this weekend. How can I avoid putting a buck in the football pool without seeming like a dork?

While office pools are illegal in some states (Wisconsin, Illinois, Hawaii, Florida), estimates are that $2.5 billion will be bet on Super Bowl games with only 30% of that in legal betting.

- The football pools might violate your state's employment laws.

- There could be problems if minors are involved or if someone outside the office participates.

- It's probably illegal if the "company" gets a cut of the kitty.

- Legal advice is needed on whether pool participants can get into harassment trouble making fun of those who don't bet.

- The pool might also be in violation of company policy; better check it out.

The bottom line, however, is this—if a pool is going on and you're not a part of it, you'll look like a dork ... period.

If it's not illegal and not against company policy, it's worth a buck to be a part of the group. Put it in your budget, and make one of your friends feel good by asking who you should root for. (One caveat—if you are morally against betting, just explain that in an objective, uncritical tone, and they probably won't ask you again).

Good hours, excellent pay, fun place to work, paid training, mean boss. Oh well, four out of five isn't bad.
[Help Wanted Ad, PA newspaper, 1994]

Mean Boss

My boss is very cordial with his peers and customers, but he's a different person with staff. Whenever he addresses one of us, he has this kind of sneer on his face and is very condescending. It makes us so mad all 10 of us are threatening to quit. Any ideas on how to deal with this?

Are you sure the problem is a condescending attitude or a cultural difference? If you're dealing with a cultural difference, you'll just need to get used to it. Don't waste your energy complaining. If opportunity arises, discuss this in positive terms, but don't let it develop into an argument.

Telling the boss he's condescending probably won't help anything. If he knows he's condescending, he'll take it as a compliment. If he doesn't know he's condescending, he won't understand what you mean.

You'll have to give him specific examples, but you'll be better off complimenting him on his style with peers and advising that employees will perform even better if he uses this same style with the home team.

If others have tried talking with him about his attitude and nothing has changed, another conversation isn't likely to get improvement. Consider what happened to those other people as you decide whether to bring up this subject. Are they still with the company? Have they been promoted (or demoted)?

Here's the bottom line. If this really bothers you, have a positive focused discussion with your boss. If things don't change, start looking for a new job. Life's too short to spend it in an abusive arrangement.

I have been complimented many times, and they
always embarrass me; I always feel that they
have not said enough.
[Mark Twain]

Never a Compliment

My boss never gives any of us any positive feedback. He's quick to tell us when something doesn't suit him, but we never hear a compliment, never even a thank you. How can we get him to understand that we're people, too?

Maybe the boss hasn't discovered that compliments instead of criticism always get better results.

Some people in our culture have the idea that if you're just doing what you're supposed to do, no compliment is deserved, even for a job well done.

Someone in your office who has a special relationship that permits direct feedback could open this subject in a non-threatening way with the boss and offer some suggestions on how to maximize productivity.

Don't criticize your boss. Instead, compliment him on what is working well. Then ask if he'd like to hear some ideas on how some managers get even better performance from staff.

You can discuss a range of ways to give positive feedback:

- Written communication: notes, memos, letters
- Awards and recognition
- Meetings and verbal feedback for individuals or teams
- Announcements and memos to compliment everyone

Trying to change this "attitude" is worth the effort, but the situation is probably not worth changing jobs if you like what you're doing and the pay is fair.

If you pick the right people and give them the
opportunity to spread their wings and put
compensation as a carrier behind it you
almost don't have to manage them.
[Jack Welch]

What Am I Worth?

The owner of our company refuses to pay us what we're worth. He keeps adding responsibilities but he will not increase pay. How do we straighten this out?

How do you know that you are worth more compensation?

Have you researched what others with similar responsibilities in your company are making?

How about the compensation of similar employees in other companies in your area?

When you have some facts to discuss, confront your boss. Be objective and company-friendly. You won't get anywhere with an aggressive attitude.

And, while you're at it, you might want to dust off that resume in case the company disagrees with your findings and discovers that they no longer need you. You knew the pay scale when you took the job.

Leaders don't create followers; they
create more leaders.
[Tom Peters]

Dangerous New Leaders

We have another new boss to train. They usually come in swinging axes and making changes. How can we get the new boss to listen to those of us who have been here for more than twenty years?

One of the primary responsibilities of a new boss is to make sure that operations continue and that good people have a chance to contribute to success.

You 20-year folks should maintain an attitude of support for the new boss; avoid negative remarks about past or present management; embrace the changes your new boss is making; get on board with the new programs or prepare your resume.

When change is necessary a new boss can minimize the stress and the errors that accompany such transitions by:

1. Finding out special talents of key leaders

2. Making sure major concerns of the leadership team are understood

3. Building confidence by helping others understand their skills and qualifications

4. Asking for more modest, routine accomplishments before raising expectations

5. Testing abilities in non-stressful situations before going after bigger goals

6. Creating enthusiasm by getting input from others

7. Taking responsibility for achievements and failures from day one

Workplace stress is as deadly as combat. It's just more
socially acceptable, and it takes longer to
die from the wounds.
[Dale Collie]

Stressors from Home

Stress from home has almost stopped all work in our office. One person's divorce is all we hear about. Another's son just got his driver's license. Somebody else has a lawsuit going on. I sympathize with their difficulties, but how can I get some productivity out of our people?

The boss is responsible for productivity and for controlling stress, regardless of its source.

You can control stress from home by having open discussions about its effect on productivity.

Set aside some time to deal with these personal issues.

Get professional help for those who need it.

Advise everyone that their personal concerns are important, but that none of you will have a job if productivity continues to slide–and that includes the boss!

Get everyone on board in trying to solve this dilemma. Ask them to hold these conversations for break and lunch time. Ask them to avoid using telephone, email, and water cooler time for these personal issues.

Demonstrate your concern. Be nice about it, but get things back on track before "unemployment" becomes part of *your* problem.

It is not the man who has little, but he who
desires more, that is poor.
[Seneca]

Sick Leave

Our state senate passed a controversial mandatory sick leave bill for companies with more than fifty employees. My complaint is that it does nothing for employees of small businesses. We get sick, too, you know. How can we make our voices heard?

When sick employees show up for work because of job dedication or because they need the pay, it's called *presenteeism*. Permitting presenteeism can actually cost companies more than paying sick individuals to stay home because they spread the illness to others.

- Federal Law requires sick leave for companies with more than fifty employees (not paid, but time off).

- The decision to have sick leave is a matter of choice for management.

- Many larger companies have a policy for paid sick leave.

- Sick leave and vacation days are key in holding onto good employees.

- Some small companies are giving employees a total number of paid days off, e.g. instead of ten vacation days and five sick leave they give 120 hours of time to be used as employee chooses.

San Francisco has an ordinance requiring paid sick leave, and California is working on a similar piece of legislature, but until the politicians catch up, we're on our own.

People who know the least always argue the most.
[American Business Observation]

Always Argumentative

What can we do about a guy in our office who is argumentative about everything. If everyone thinks it's too cold in here, he thinks it's too hot. If we get a day off, he gripes about management's bad judgment. If we get a big order, he complains about the sales people. Any ideas on what we can do about his attitude?

Negative people drag everyone else down. They ruin the day for everyone in the office and everyone who comes into contact with them. Their attitudes affect everyone's productivity.

Sometimes we meet people who use negative remarks in a humorous way, but I don't think that's what we're talking about here.

Another real possibility is that this person's negativity is the result of *too much stress*.

We don't have enough background to understand the source of this person's stress, whether it's workplace stress or something external, but if the problem is stress, this person would benefit from some professional counseling.

Management needs to discuss the issue with this negative individual. Find out what is needed:

- Teamwork - attitude adjustment
- Stress control - internal or external
- Anger management—if the level of argument has reached this level

If workplace stress is the issue, it can be damaging to both individuals and the company.

A melody is not merely something you can hum.
[Aaron Copeland]

Whistling and Humming

Is there anything I can do about the guy in the next cube who constantly whistles and hums while he works? I'm glad he's happy, but this is driving me crazy and affecting my work.

It's nice to know that you have happiness right in the next cube! But, it's easy to see how this can be annoying if it is constant.

You need to approach this in the right way so you don't insult your co-worker. Your conversation needs to be about the whistling and humming, not about him.

How about going into his cube when he's not on deadline and asking if you can talk about something that's on your mind? He'll say, "OK." Then you explain in a very friendly (with plenty of smiling and relaxed posture) that you need to ask a favor.

Very objectively tell him that you're glad he is so happy, but his happiness is interfering with your productivity. Laugh when you say this. Tell him he is very good whistler and you enjoy the tunes he hums, but it is kind of distracting.

He will apologize, and that will probably be the end of it. The next time you hear the music from the next cube, you can jokingly comment about his "joy" being out of control again. Laugh with him about it.

If the conversation doesn't work at all, get a headset with some great music to cover the sounds he makes. Then, you'll both be happy.

You don't want to diminish this guy's happiness or productivity, so be careful with this.

I never forget a face, but in your case, I'll
gladly make an exception.
[Groucho Marks]

Forgetful

One of my sales people frequently misspeaks. He'll say one customer's name when he means another. He says the wrong product names when he full well knows the difference. And a couple of times he has flatly declared that he was not present at a conversation when I know that he was. What's going on with this otherwise great employee?

One of the signs of excessive workplace stress is forgetfulness, and this includes misspeaking words without realizing it.

You can do a lot to control workplace stress with good communication and leadership.

- First thing, have a conversation about work topics to see if there is any mention of overload or inability to get everything done he'd like to do.

- Bring up home topics and see if there's any conversation about stress from home that can be affecting his work.

- Also, consider whether a little time off is in order – a week's vacation can do wonders for workplace stress.

- Learn how leaders can control workplace stress, improve productivity, and reduce the impact of stress on employees. As said elsewhere, workplace stress is a leadership responsibility.

- Find a good resource on this topic through Amazon or your book store.

Whoever gossips to you will gossip about you.
[Spanish Proverb]

Gossip

How can we get people to quit gossiping so much at work? We lose a lot of time because people are talking about each other, and a lot of damage is done by false rumors that come out of it. Any ideas?

If you're a manager, one of your responsibilities is making sure everyone is on task. Be careful about bringing up this topic if you're not in management because controlling the work habits of other employees is probably not in your job description. Excessive gossip reduces productivity, and employees can actually sue companies for allowing malicious gossip to continue.

Some actions that can be taken include:

- Improving communications from management

- Informing employees that malicious gossip won't be tolerated

- Including this topic in the company policy manual

- Making people aware of these dangers in multiple communications: policy manual, bulletin board posters, individual memos, and personal letters from the president

- Making sure everyone has enough work (busy employees are less likely to gossip)

You can personally tell others that you don't want to hear the gossip and refuse to pass it along when you become aware of it. You can even discuss this topic with the source when you're sure of your facts. But, remember, if you're not in management, you need to leave the broader topic for their attention.

Your 2 Cents!

What's driving you crazy at the office? Tell everyone what bothers you, why you can't get your work done, what's unfair, or your own ideas on how to handle any of those you read about in *Last Nerve*.

Send your own 2¢ worth to
LastNerve@CourageBuilders.com

More Books by Dale Collie

Frontline Leadership: From War Room to Boardroom

Building Courageous Leaders

Winning under Fire: Turn Stress into Success the US Army Way

Campfires & Gun Smoke: Vietnam Company Commander

Professional Speaker

As a professional speaker Dale Collie uses the leadership skills of US Army Rangers to help key people succeed in tough times. Check out Dale's web site; follow him on social media, or contact him for more information at

www.sn.im/contact-dale
www.CourageBuilders.com